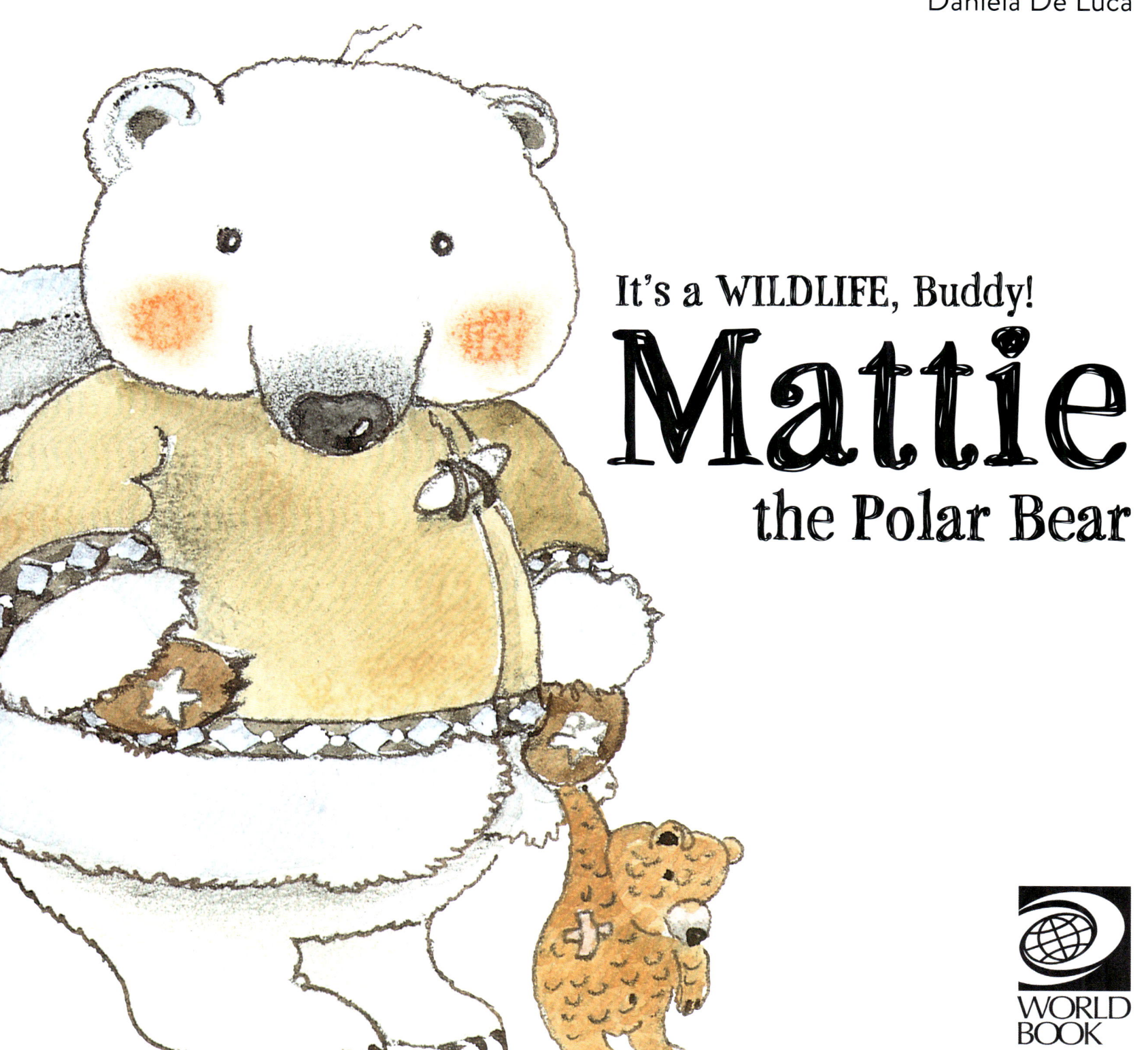

Daniela De Luca

It's a WILDLIFE, Buddy!

Mattie

the Polar Bear

WORLD BOOK

World Book, Inc.
180 North LaSalle Street
Suite 900
Chicago, Illinois 60601
USA

For school and library sales, please phone
1-800-975-3250 (United States)
or 1-800-837-5365 (Canada).

www.worldbook.com

Copyright © 2017 by Nextquisite Ltd, London
Publishers: Anne McRae, Marco Nardi
www.nextquisite.com

All illustrations by Daniela De Luca
Texts: Daniela De Luca, Anne McRae, Neil Morris
Editing: Anne McRae, Vicky Egan, Neil Morris
Graphic Design: Marco Nardi
Layout: Marco Nardi, Rebecca Milner

This edition edited and revised by World Book, Inc.
by permission of Nextquisite Ltd.

ISBN: 978-0-7166-3519-2 (set), 978-0-7166-3526-0 (Mattie the Polar Bear)

Printed and bound in China
1st printing March 2017

LIBRARY OF CONGRESS
CATALOGING-IN-PUBLICATION DATA
HAS BEEN APPLIED FOR.

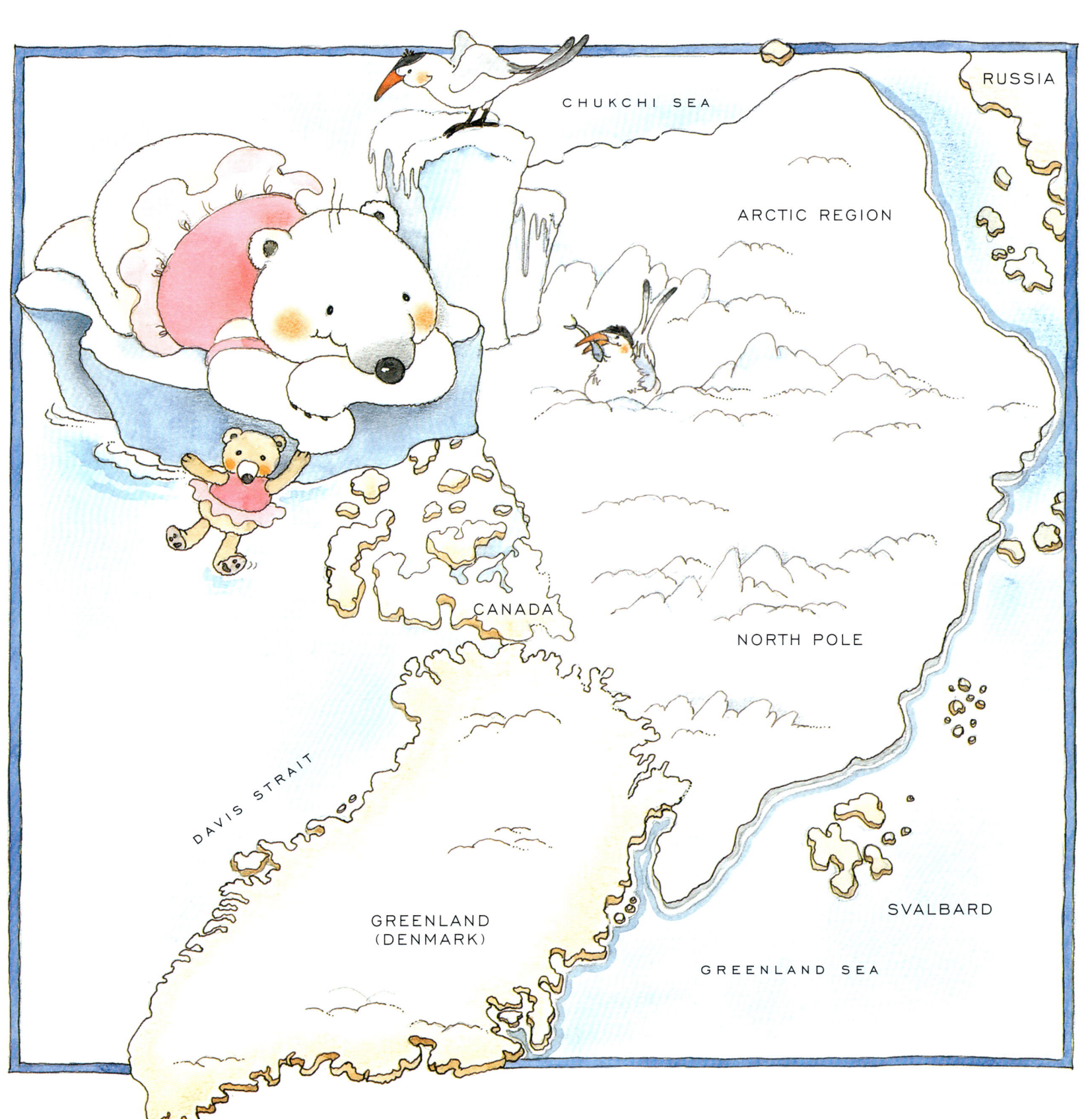

CHUKCHI SEA

RUSSIA

ARCTIC REGION

CANADA

NORTH POLE

DAVIS STRAIT

GREENLAND
(DENMARK)

SVALBARD

GREENLAND SEA

DO POLAR BEARS SLEEP ALL WINTER?

Adult females sleep during winter if they will be giving birth to cubs (babies). They dig a den in a snowdrift, sleep there most of the time, and then give birth to their cubs in November or December. The cozy den is a safe and warm home for the cubs. Male polar bears and females that are not having cubs are active all year round.

MOTHER POLAR BEAR WAKES UP with a start. She has had a long sleep and wonders what day or even month it is. "Well, it's certainly later than 9 o'clock, and little Mattie will want her breakfast," she thinks. But her cub is still fast asleep. "I'd better check if we've got any food left. I haven't been out all winter," Mother growls to herself.

HOME
SWEET
HOME

5

WHILE THE BEARS WERE ASLEEP in their den, spring has come to Arctic Island. Mrs. Ermine is taking her children for a walk in the snow. "Don't play around the polar bear's den," she warns them. But Ernie disobeys and shows off his new sliding skills when his mother's not looking.

ARE ALL POLAR BEAR DENS THE SAME?

They vary in shape and size, and they even change as wind blows fresh snow over the top. In very windy places, there may be a mound of snow over the entrance to the den.

WHERE IN THE WORLD DO POLAR BEARS LIVE?

Polar bears live in the **Arctic** region. This is the area of frozen sea around the **North Pole**. The bears live mainly at the edge of the **pack ice**.

O<small>H</small> <small>DEAR</small>, there's nothing in the den to eat, only a few old fish bones. "That won't be enough to feed a growing cub," says Mother Bear. Just then Mattie wakes up. "I'm starving," she yawns. "What's for breakfast?"

R<small>INGED</small> <small>SEALS</small>

E<small>GGS</small>

B<small>IRD</small>

K<small>ELP</small>

WHAT DO POLAR BEARS EAT?
Newborn cubs drink their mother's milk. When they are older, polar bears' main food is ringed seal. They also hunt lemmings, voles, and small birds, as well as walrus pups.

V<small>OLE</small>

L<small>EMMING</small>

W<small>ALRUS</small> <small>PUP</small>

ARE POLAR BEAR CUBS REALLY TINY?

Yes, they are much smaller than other animals at birth when compared to the size of their mother. Cubs are born blind and deaf, and they have very thin fur. Their mother keeps them warm.

DO POLAR BEAR MOTHERS HAVE TWINS?

Yes, in fact most polar bear births are of twins. Some mothers have a single cub, and occasionally they have triplets.

MOTHER BEAR TELLS MATTIE that they have to go to Wally Walrus's store to buy food. "We'd better wrap up warm," she says, zipping up the cub's jacket.

BEFORE THEY SET OFF, Mother has a quick look in the mirror. She's pleased with her new green coat. When they make their way across the ice, it creaks under their paws.

WHY DON'T POLAR BEARS SLIP ON THE ICE?

Because their big paws act like snowshoes. They have short, sharp claws and fur padding, which give them a good grip on ice and snow.

11

WALLY WALRUS IS BUSY TODAY. He's in a good mood, handing out candy and telling everyone proudly that he has just become a father. "Could we see the little pup?" Mother Bear asks politely. "Of course!" Wally says.

THEY ARE NOT the only visitors.
Mrs. Seal has come with her daughter
Sissy to show her own new pup.

Mother Bear congratulates the other mothers, and then they
catch up on the island news. Mattie and Sissy soon get bored.
"Let's go play in the snow," Mattie whispers, and the two
youngsters quietly sneak out of the room.

ARE POLAR BEARS GOOD SWIMMERS?

Yes, adults are strong swimmers and can cover long distances without resting. Their small head and long neck give them a streamlined shape. They can also swim underwater for up to two minutes.

HOW DO POLAR BEARS GET DRY?

After swimming, they shake themselves, and their thick fur throws the water off.

OUT ON THE ICE, Mattie tells Sissy that she is learning **ballet**. "I'll show you," she says, taking off her jacket. To Sissy's surprise Mattie is all dressed up, ready to dance. In her pink outfit she looks like a real ballerina.

14

MATTIE DOES A ROLY-POLY leap, a pretty spin, and some big jumps. She glides along on tiptoe, when suddenly there is a loud cracking noise. A block of ice breaks away and takes Mattie with it.

"Oh, no!" Sissy cries out.

15

WHAT IS AN ICEBERG?

Icebergs are huge chunks of ice that break off from glaciers and ice shelves. They float away, and only the top part shows above the water. Most of the iceberg is under the water's surface.

WHITE WHALE

MATTIE FLOATS AWAY on the ice and is soon out of sight. Her mother is horrified when she sees what has happened. "Oh dear, I don't know who can save her now," says Grandma Arctic Hare. "Oh dear, neither do I," says Grandpa Hare.

GRANDPA AND
GRANDMA
ARCTIC HARE

THE HOODED SEALS try to help, but all they can catch is Mattie's teddy bear. Mattie grabs it and floats on. "Too much dancing," says Mr. Arctic Wolf. "Too near the edge," says Mrs. Arctic Fox. "What drama!" screech the terns as they fly overhead.

HARRY AND HANNA
HOODED SEAL

18

MR. WOLF

MRS. FOX

19

WHAT ARE THE DANGERS FOR CUBS?

A fall on the ice might injure a polar bear cub. If it breaks a bone, it might not be able to keep up with its mother. It needs to stay close, because adult male bears sometimes kill cubs.

PAMELA, PATRICK, AND PIERRE PUFFIN

THE PUFFINS CAN SEE that Mattie is now in real danger.
A gigantic, growling polar bear rears up on his hind
legs and lifts a powerful paw. He looks ready to swallow
Mattie and her teddy in a single mouthful.

21

LUCKILY THE STRONG OCEAN CURRENT floats Mattie out of reach of the huge growling bear. But before she knows it, she crashes into a big gray mountain rising up out of the sea. "Maybe it's a new Arctic island," Mattie thinks.

DO POLAR BEARS REALLY TRAVEL ON ICE FLOES?

Yes, in the summer adult polar bears follow the shifting pack ice as it melts into floes, or sheets of floating ice. Sometimes blocks of ice break away, so females keep an eye on their cubs and keep them close.

"THIS ISLAND IS VERY SOFT," Mattie thinks, "and very slippery too!" She just manages to hold on to the moving island.

BUT IT'S NOT AN ISLAND AT ALL! Lucky Mattie sees that she has been saved by an old friend of her mother's. She's a helpful whale, and she knows these waters well. "You can call me Auntie Birgit," she tells Mattie. "Now, let's get you home."

MOTHER BEAR AND HER FRIENDS are so pleased to see Mattie safe and well. Sissy Seal claps her flippers, as Mattie takes a bow. Mother can't wait to give her little cub a great big furry cuddle.

HOW LONG DO CUBS STAY WITH THEIR MOTHER?

Cubs stay close to their mother at all times until they are about two or two and a half years old. By then they have learned to hunt, and they may go off on their own.

LATER, BACK IN THEIR DEN, Mother
Bear reads her cub a bedtime story.
Mattie is so happy in her mother's
arms that she falls asleep long
before the story's happy ending.

DID YOU KNOW?

There are various species, or kinds, of bear. They live in many different parts of the world, from the Arctic region to areas of North and South America, Europe, and Asia. The grizzly bear is a type of brown bear.

POLAR BEAR

POLAR BEAR CUB

AMERICAN BLACK BEAR

BROWN BEARS

Grizzly bear

Sun bear

Sloth bear

Asiatic black bear

Spectacled bear

Here is Mattie with some of her friends. They all live in the Arctic region, at the top of the world near the North Pole. Where is Mattie? Do you recognize all her friends?

Bowhead whale

Narwhal

Polar bear

Puffin

Hooded seal

Arctic wolf

Snowy owl

Eider duck

30

MATTIE (AND TEDDY)

ARCTIC TERN

Fully grown polar bears are big and strong. But they and other wild animals need help from people to have enough space to live and be kept safe from hunters. Areas of the ice where polar bears live and hunt are melting. Earth is getting warmer because of people's activities, such as burning coal, that can change the climate.

WALRUS

MUSK OX

RIBBON SEAL

BELUGA (WHITE) WHALE

WEASEL

ARCTIC HARE

LEMMING

ARCTIC FOX

31

Glossary

Terms defined in this glossary are in type that **looks like this** (bold type) on their first appearance on any two facing pages (a spread).

Arctic - the northernmost region of Earth surrounding the North Pole and including northern parts of North America, Europe, and Asia

ballet - a type of dance that uses special movements and poses, or postures, that are graceful and elegant

North Pole - a term used for an invisible point on Earth's surface in the Arctic region. The North Pole is a point in the center of the Arctic Ocean where all Earth's lines of longitude meet. Lines of longitude mark distances east and west on Earth's surface

pack ice - large areas of ice made up of chunks of ice, or floes, that have frozen together

Note to the Grown-Ups: Each "It's a Wildlife, Buddy!" book combines a whimsical narrative and factual background information to help children learn a little life lesson and a few things about some animals with which we share the world. We have the animal characters say and do things that are not possible for them in the wild to create stories that can appeal to children and that they can relate to. The stories can help children think about making friends, growing up, and other important parts of their lives. The fanciful stories are balanced by basic facts about the animals' lives and behaviors in nature. This combination creates a satisfying and informing reading experience whether an adult is reading to a child or a child is reading on his or her own.